WHAT BUMOSAUR IS THAT?

ANDY GRIFFITHS & TERRY DENTON

MACMILLAN CHILDREN'S BOOKS

First published in a smaller format black and white paperback
in 2007 by Pan Macmillan Australia Pty Limited
and Macmillan Children's Books

This hardback colour edition first published in 2007
by Macmillan Children's Books
a division of Macmillan Publishers Limited
The Macmillan Building, 4 Crinan Street, London N1 9XW
Basingstoke and Oxford
Associated companies throughout the world
www.panmacmillan.com

ISBN 978-0-330-45732-3

Contents

Introduction

Life on Earth began with primitive bumteria that appeared in the oceans during the Pre-Crappian time, 600 million years ago. Over time, these bumteria bumvolved into more complex forms of bum life, including invertebutts, bumfish, bumphibians, stenchtiles, farthropods and stinksects, until eventually giving rise to the group of stenchtiles we know as the bumosaurs and bumornithids.

Bumosaurs appeared on the Earth 250 million years ago at the beginning of the Triarssic period. They came in a stunning variety of shapes and sizes, with an equally stunning variety of stinks and stenches.

Dominating bum life on Earth for the next 185 million years, bumosaurs disappeared from the fossil record around 65 million years ago. (Though it has been speculated that some very exceptional exceptions survived.) The exstinktion of the bumosaurs allowed a new species of bum life called bummals to bumvolve, eventually leading to the emergence of the earliest bum-men.

Although the focus of this book is on bumosaurs, examples of bum-related life forms from all major groups have been included in order to provide the most comprehensive — and up-to-date — guide to prehistoric bum life ever published.

Bumolutionary time-chart

PRE-CRAPPIAN TIME
4600–540 million years ago (mya)
Origin of bum life in the sea

CRAPOZOIC ERA

CRAPPIAN PERIOD
540–500 mya
First invertebutts

ORDUNGOCIAN PERIOD
500–435 mya
First vertebutts (bumfish) and bum-plants

SEWERIAN PERIOD
435–410 mya
Armoured bumfish

DEBUMIAN PERIOD
410–355 mya
First bumphibians

CARBUMIFEROUS PERIOD
355–295 mya
First stinksects and farthropods

POOMIAN PERIOD
First stenchtiles
295–250 mya

MESSOZOIC ERA

TRIARSSIC PERIOD
First bumosaurs
250–203 mya

JURARSSIC PERIOD
First flying bumosaurs
203–135 mya

CRAPACEOUS PERIOD
135–65 mya
First gigantic bumosaurs

SCENTOZOIC ERA

FARTOCENE EPOCH
65–1.75 mya
First bummals

BUMOCENE EPOCH
1.75 mya –present
First Bumanderthals and bum-men

From Invertebutts, Bumfish, Bumphibians and Stenchtiles to Farthropods and Stinksects

Life on Earth began in the seas with primitive bumteria during the Pre-crappian time. Eventually, these early single-cheeked bums clumped together to form some of the first multi-cheeked invertebutts in the Crapozoic era oceans.

Next, major advances in bumolution during the Crapozoic era saw the rise of the first vertebutts (bum life forms with internal skeletons). During the Ordungocian period (500–435 million years ago) the first bumfish appeared and soon bumvolved into an astonishing variety of forms that quickly came to dominate the prehistoric seas.

Then, around 400 million years ago, using their fins as primitive limbs, some of the more adventurous bumfish crawled on to land to take up residence in the abundant swamps and bogs of the Crapozoic era. The descendants of these brave pooineers bumvolved into the first bumphibians and then stenchtiles.

And hot on the heels of the bumphibians, sea-dwelling invertebutts rapidly bumvolved their own creeping, crawling, flying and farting armies to invade the land – farthropods and stinksects.

INVERTEBUTTS –
TRILOBUTT

SEA SCORPIBUM

OCTOBUMOPUS

BUMFISH –
BUM-HEAD SHARK

DEEP-SEA BUM-DANGLER

BUMPHIBIANS AND STENCHTILES –
BUMSKIPPER

POOPIGATOR

TURDLE

FARTHROPODS AND STINKSECTS –
GIANT MUTANT BLOWFLY

BUMANTULA

Invertebutt: Trilobutt

Appearing some 600 million years ago, the Trilobutt was a hard, triple-cheeked bottom feeder. Its flattened shape made it uniquely suited to filtering mud, invertebutt droppings and bumganic particles as it scuttled along the sea floor.

Its hard shell kept it safe from predators; thus it was one of the most successful of all early bum life forms. It swam, crawled and burrowed in the Crapozoic oceans for the next 350 million years.

There were many different species of Trilobutt, and some — such as *Trilobuttus gigantis* — grew to enormarse proportions.

VITAL STATISTICS

Scientific name: *Tricheekium buttus*
Family: Stinkerbutt
Diet: Mudivorarse
Time: Crapozoic era 540–250 mya
Stink rating: 💩💩💩💩💩

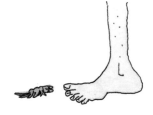

Invertebutt:
Sea scorpibum

The Sea scorpibum was the giant ancestor of
the modern-day scorpion, and one of the most
feared prehistoric deep-water bum life forms. The
enormous claws of a Sea scorpibum could cut
a giant Trilobutt in half, and the venom-sacs in
its bum-shaped stinger contained raw sewage so
potent it could kill a school of Jelly bumfish within
seconds.

Evidence suggests, however, that these terrifying
creatures engaged in quite elegant courtship rituals.
These would begin with the male grasping the
female's pincers and performing a dance called the
bumenade a deux. This dance eventually developed
into a range of styles, including bumroom dancing,
bum-ballet, stench-jazz and stink-hop.

VITAL STATISTICS

Scientific name: *Scorpius oceania*
Family: Pinchabutt
Diet: Carnivorarse
Time: Ordungocian, Sewerian 500–410 mya
Stink rating: ♣ ♣ ♣ ♣ ♣

9

Invertebutt: Octobumopus

The eight-armed, eight-headed, sixteen-cheeked, sixteen-eyed Octobumopus was a predecessor of the eight-armed, one-headed, two-eyed octopus that we are familiar with today.

As well as being bizarre in appearance, the Octobumopus had a highly developed defence system. If threatened, it would eject eight clouds of thick brownish liquid to blind – and disgust – predators. It would then use the incredible thrusting power of its sixteen cheeks to escape at high speed, leaving its attacker completely grossed out and in desperate need of an industrial-strength disinfectant.

VITAL STATISTICS

Scientific name: *Octavio posteriosi*
Family: Freakasaur
Diet: Carnivorarse
Time: Sewerian 435–410 mya
Stink rating: 🐾🐾🐾

Bumfish:
Bum-head shark

A close relative of the better known – and still existing – Hammer-head shark, the Bum-head shark suffered from very low self-esteem due to the fact that everyone called it a bum-head. Which was true, but nevertheless very hurtful. For instance, how would you like it if everybody called you a bum-head? It would be hurtful enough even if you didn't have a bum-head . . . but imagine how much more it would hurt if you did.

It was perhaps the hurtful nature of this taunt that accounted for the extraordinary frequency and severity of Bum-head shark attacks during the Carbumiferous period.

So the Bum-head shark teaches us an important lesson: be kind to others . . . even if they act like bum-heads, and especially if they do have a bum-shaped head.

VITAL STATISTICS

Scientific name: *Bum-headius maximus*
Family: Bumshark
Diet: Carnivorarse
Time: Carbumiferous 355–295 mya
Stink rating: ✿✿✿✿✿

Bumfish:
Deep-sea bum-dangler

The Deep-sea bum-dangler got its name from the bioluminescent bum that dangled from its dorsal spine. Millions of light-producing bumteria caused this false bum to glow a blue-green colour. These colourful lures came in a variety of styles and no two were the same. Some had flashing pimples; others had warts capable of impressive strobe-lighting effects.

The Deep-sea bum-dangler used its false bum to attract prey. It would wiggle the false bum in front of its large, fang-packed mouth. Then, when its fascinated, almost hypnotized, prey moved close enough, the Deep-sea bum-dangler would flick its dangling bum out of the way and snap up the prey in its powerful jaws.

VITAL STATISTICS

Scientific name: *Dangleri prosthetica*
Family: Freakafish
Diet: Bumfishivorarse
Time: Carbumiferous 355–295 mya
Stink rating:

Bumphibian: Bumskipper

The Bumskipper was one of the first true bumphibians, able to live both in and out of the water. On land the Bumskipper moved along the bog shores by 'skipping' on its bum-shaped fins.

Living on land gave the Bumskipper tremendous advantages, the most important of which was the ability to release gas in private without the embarrassing telltale bubbles that accompany it in water. Of course, releasing gas above water meant the noises that often accompany the action could be heard clearly for the first time. These noises, however, were deemed so amusing that the Bumskipper was happy to give up its recently won privacy, and rapidly developed the full range of expressive sound effects that bums still employ – and enjoy so much – today.

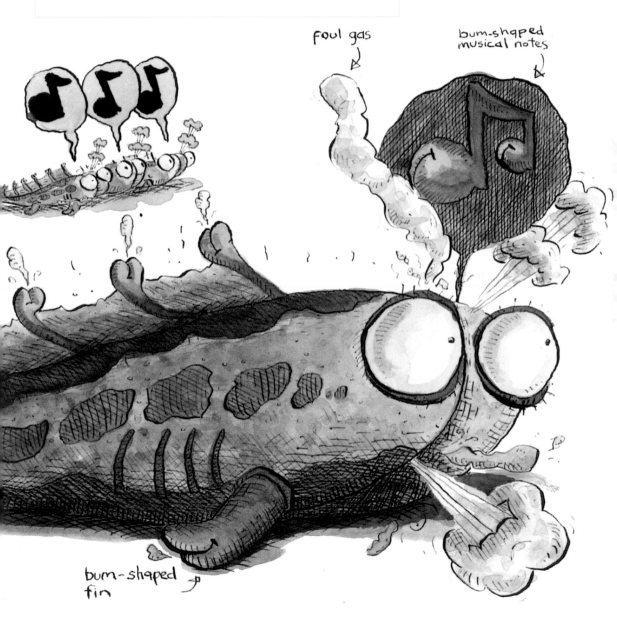

VITAL STATISTICS

Scientific name: *Tetratis poddus*
Family: Stinkophibian
Diet: Herbivorarse
Time: Debumian 410–355 mya
Stink rating: 🐾🐾🐾

foul gas

bum-shaped
musical notes

bum-shaped
fin

Stenchtile: Poopigator

The Poopigator bore a strong resemblance to the modern alligator, only it was much bigger, much browner and much, much smellier. While its appearance was quite threatening, the Poopigator's breath was far worse than its bite. Nevertheless, its bite was still quite bad.

The Poopigator consumed large prey by dragging it into a bog and then spinning or convulsing wildly until bite-size pieces were torn off. This is referred to as the 'deathbog roll' – not to be confused with 'bog roll', which is slang for toilet paper.

VITAL STATISTICS

Scientific name: *Poopius gatori*
Family: Crapotile
Diet: Omnivorarse, Bogivorarse
Time: Poomian 295–250 mya
Stink rating: ✿✿✿✿✿

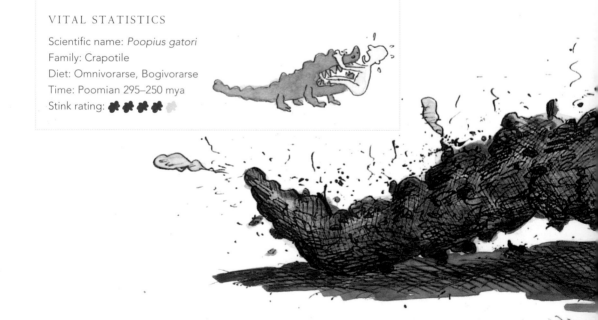

Stenchtile: Turdle

The Turdle was the slowest and most timid of all stenchtiles and is thought to be a predecessor of modern tortoises and turtles as it has features in common with both species.

At the first sign of danger the Turdle would pull in its arms, legs, neck and head so it would appear to be just a piece of poo, virtually indistinguishable from all the other millions of pieces of poo on the ground . . . or were they other Turdles engaged in a similar defence strategy?

This form of camouflage was so successful that often a Turdle would not be able to tell the difference between a piece of poo and a fellow member of its own species. As a result Turdles would often make the tragic mistake of selecting a poo rather than a Turdle as a lifetime partner.

VITAL STATISTICS

Scientific name: *Turdi domesticus*
Family: Turdotile
Diet: Herbivorarse, Bogivorarse
Time: Triarssic 250–203 mya
Stink rating: 🐾🐾🐾🐾🐾

Farthropod: Bumantula

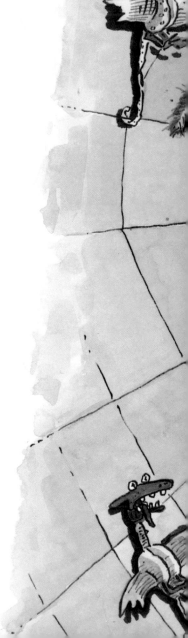

The Bumantula had an enormarse abdobum, eight beady brown eyes, two terrifying sharp fangs and eight powerful legs. The bum-web built by this prehistoric, spider-like Freakapod was made up of long brown strands of bum silk. These bum-webs were strong enough to catch large stinksects, as well as flying bumosaurs, such as Bumadactyls and Pteranobums.

While the Bumantula remained largely unchanged for almost 200 million years, the species did not exist in large numbers, due to the fact that most Bumantulas were scared of each other. And with good reason — attempts at mating often resulted in both Bumantulas crushing and stenching each other to death.

VITAL STATISTICS

Scientific name: *Posterius terribulus*
Family: Freakapod
Diet: Carnivorarse
Time: Messozoic era 250–65 mya
Stink rating: ✿ ✿ ✿ ✿ ✿

Stinksect:
Giant mutant blowfly

While not technically a bumosaur itself, the Giant mutant blowfly was the constant companion of bumosaurs, thriving on both their waste products and their carcasses.

One million times bigger than its modern counterpart, the Giant mutant blowfly was also one million times more annoying. It liked to spray large quantities of yellowy-green goo out of its bumboscis, suck the head off its prey and lay Giant mutant maggots in the unfortunate victim's neck-hole.

While able to adapt successfully to any place where bumosaurs lived, the Giant mutant maggot grew especially gigantic in enclosed environments, such as bumcanoes and underground caves (also known as maggotoriums).

VITAL STATISTICS

Scientific name: *Mutatis blowflyus*
Family: Disgustosect
Diet: Omnivorarse
Time: Carbumiferous, Poomian, Triarssic 355–203 mya
Stink rating: ✿ ✿ ✿ ✿ ✿

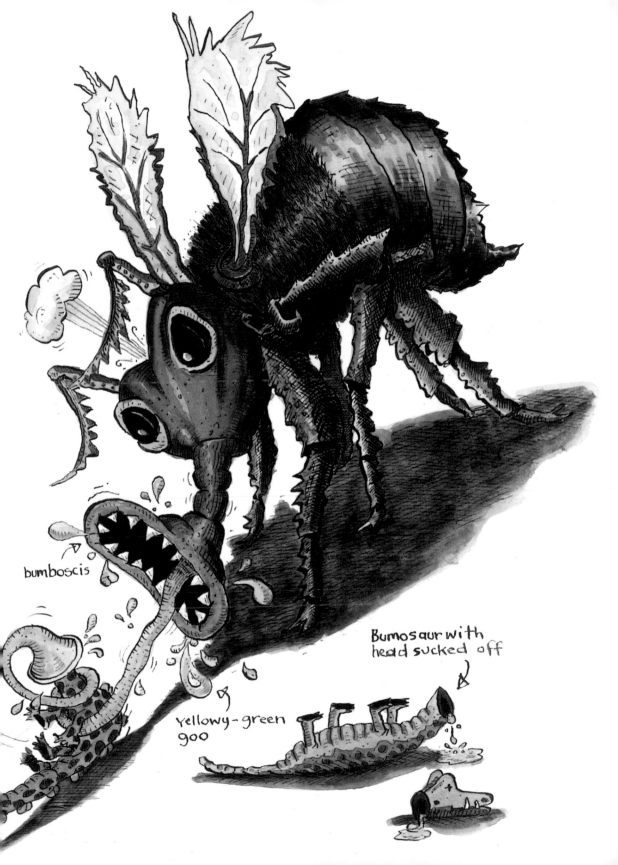

bumboscis

yellowy-green goo

Bumosaur with head sucked off

Bumolution: how life bumvolved

Life on Earth began with bumteria that appeared in the oceans 600 million years ago. Over time, these bumteria bumvolved into more complex forms of bum life until eventually giving rise to the group of stenchtiles we know as the bumosaurs. The exstinktion of the bumosaurs around 65 million years ago allowed a new species of bum life called bummals to bumvolve, eventually leading to the emergence of the earliest bum-men.

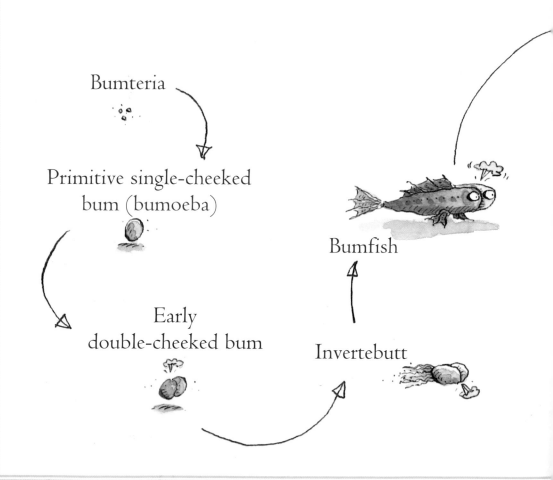

Bumteria

Primitive single-cheeked bum (bumoeba)

Bumfish

Early double-cheeked bum

Invertebutt

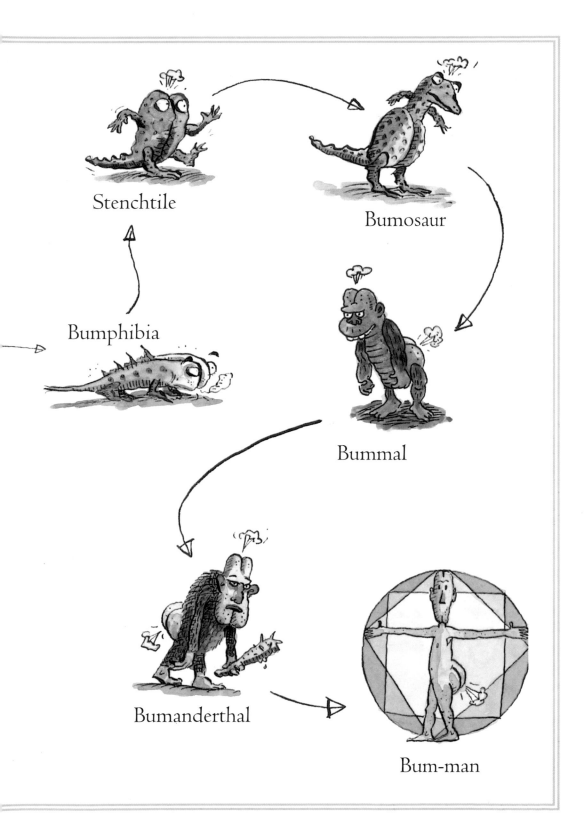

Stenchtile

Bumosaur

Bumphibia

Bummal

Bumanderthal

Bum-man

Toiletrollasaurus Bum-headed idiotasaurus Very
droopy-eyed idiotasaurus Bum-eyed bumosaurus
Skullbuttosaurus Sparebumosaurus Stink Kong
white bumosaurus Microbumosaurus Stenchganto
long-legged short-tailed stupid-looking tiny bum-h
Diapersaurus Diarrhoeasaurus Frill-necked cyclop
Tricerabutt Tyrannosore-arse rex Bigarseosaurus
Toiletrollasaurus Bum-headed idiotasaurus Very
droopy-eyed idiotasaurus Bum-eyed bumosaurus
Skullbuttosaurus Sparebumosaurus Stink Kong
white bumosaurus Microbumosaurus Stenchganto
long-legged short-tailed stupid-looking tiny bum-h
Diapersaurus Diarrhoeasaurus Frill-necked cyclop
Tricerabutt Tyrannosore-arse rex Bigarseosaurus
Toiletrollasaurus Bum-headed idiotasaurus Very
droopy-eyed idiotasaurus Bum-eyed bumosaurus
Skullbuttosaurus Sparebumosaurus Stink Kong
white bumosaurus Microbumosaurus Stenchganto
long-legged short-tailed stupid-looking tiny bum-h
Diapersaurus Diarrhoeasaurus Frill-necked cyclop
Tricerabutt Tyrannosore-arse rex Bigarseosaurus
Toiletrollasaurus Bum-headed idiotasaurus Very
droopy-eyed idiotasaurus Bum-eyed bumosaurus
Skullbuttosaurus Sparebumosaurus Stink Kong
white bumosaurus Microbumosaurus Stenchganto
long-legged short-tailed stupid-looking tiny bum-h
Diapersaurus Diarrhoeasaurus Frill-necked cyclop
Tricerabutt Tyrannosore-arse rex Bigarseosaurus
Toiletrollasaurus Bum-headed idiotasaurus Very
droopy-eyed idiotasaurus Bum-eyed bumosaurus
Skullbuttosaurus Sparebumosaurus Stink Kong
white bumosaurus Microbumosaurus Stenchganto

Bumosaurs

The Messozoic era saw the rise of some of the best-known, most aggressive and most stupid members of the bumosaur family.

TOILETROLLASAURUS

BUM-HEADED IDIOTASAURUS

VERY RARE LONG-NECKED LONG-LEGGED SHORT-TAILED STUPID-LOOKING TINY BUM-HEADED DROOPY-EYED IDIOTASAURUS

BUM-EYED BUMOSAURUS

BUMONTOPIMUS

DIAPERSAURUS

DIARRHOEASAURUS

FRILL-NECKED CYCLOPOOTOPS

SKULLBUTTOSAURUS

SPAREBUMOSAURUS

STINK KONG

TOILETBRUSHASAURUS

TRICERABUTT

TYRANNOSORE-ARSE REX

BIGARSEOSAURUS

GREAT WHITE BUMOSAURUS

MICROBUMOSAURUS

STENCHGANTORSAURUS

Toiletrollasaurus

The Toiletrollasaurus appeared in a dazzling variety of colours, patterns and textures. Also known as the 'Bogrollasaurus', the various sub-species differed immensely in size, weight, tear-ability, softness, 'finger-breakthrough' resistance and degrees of absorption.

Despite these differences, they shared one common feature: a permanent expression of terror due to the fact that they were preyed upon by almost every other type of bumosaur. The Toiletrollasaurus was widely hunted because it was prized for its long, soft, absorbent tail. It is thought that the perforations on the Toiletrollasaurus's tail bumvolved as a defence against its many predators. Like some species of modern-day lizard, if caught by the tail it could lose a section and then regrow it.

VITAL STATISTICS

Scientific name: *Papyrus posteri*
Family: Wipeosaur
Diet: Herbivorarse
Time: Messozoic era 250–65 mya
Stink rating:

Upsidedown spotted Toiletrollasaurus

two-headed Toiletrollasaurus

handy six pack Toiletrollasaurus

Bum-headed idiotasaurus

Consisting of one large bum with a smaller bum-head atop a long, slug-like neck, the Bum-headed idiotasaurus was idiotic in both appearance and behaviour.

Like most idiots, it spent its time doing idiotic and dangerous things, such as swimming in quicksand-like bum-bogs, playing on the edges of active bumcanoes and running across busy roads without looking.

Not surprisingly, perhaps, bumosaurologists have found a number of fossil graveyards in which groups of Bum-headed idiotasauruses appear to have died and been buried together.

VITAL STATISTICS

Scientific name: *Dumbumius minor*
Family: Stupidosaur
Diet: Herbivorarse
Time: Triarssic 250–203 mya
Stink rating:

Very rare long-necked long-legged short-tailed stupid-looking tiny bum-headed droopy-eyed idiotasaurus

The Very rare long-necked long-legged short-tailed stupid-looking tiny bum-headed droopy-eyed idiotasaurus was very rare due to the fact that it was too stupid to eat, drink, find shelter or even mate. If it did manage to reproduce, it was usually by accident.

In fact, the only interesting fact about the Very rare long-necked long-legged short-tailed stupid-looking tiny bum-headed droopy-eyed idiotasaurus is that it had the longest and stupidest-sounding name of all the bumosaurs.

VITAL STATISTICS

Scientific name: Dumbumius major
Family: Stupidosaur
Diet: Too dumb to eat
Time: Triarssic 250–203 mya
Stink rating:

Bum-eyed bumosaurus

Five eyes, six legs and twelve bum cheeks made the Bum-eyed bumosaurus one of the more bizarre and dangerous bumosaurs.

It could see in five directions at the same time and its six legs allowed it to cover vast distances very quickly. Its multiple cheeks also allowed it to produce five times as much gas as other similar-sized bumosaurs. It used this gas to stun its victims before eating them.

So the Bum-eyed bumosaurus was an excellent hunter and well protected from attack by other predators. In fact, the only creature the Bum-eyed bumosaurus had to fear was itself as it was very easy for a Bum-eyed bumosaurus to get its five necks in a knot and accidentally strangle itself to death.

VITAL STATISTICS

Scientific name: *Stupido stupendius*
Family: Freakabutt
Diet: Carnivorarse
Time: Triarssic 250–203 mya
Stink rating: 🌸🌸🌸🌸

Bumontopimus

Bumontopimus spent most of its time stumbling around, holding its 'head' and trying to think of what to do next. This, of course, was impossible because its 'head' was in fact a bum, and as such it had no brain. The lack of a brain meant that it also had no memory, thus it often forgot that it had no brain, which is why it continued to spend so much of its time holding its 'head' and trying to think.

The sheer stupidity of the Bumontopimus made it an obvious target for any bumosaur looking for an easy meal and thus the species sadly became exstinkt quite soon after it first appeared. Not that it really mattered – Bumontopimuses were too stupid to know that they had even existed in the first place.

VITAL STATISTICS

Scientific name: Butterius cranium
Family: Stupidosaur
Diet: Can't remember to eat
Time: Triarssic 250–203 mya
Stink rating:

Diapersaurus

Coming in two main species, Cloth and Disposable, the small, highly intelligent Diapersaurus would attach itself to a new-born bumosaur of another species. This arrangement was beneficial to both parties. The Diapersaurus was provided with nourishment and protection from other large bumosaurs, and the young bumosaur was protected from the harsh conditions of the prehistoric bumosaur world.

These relationships were usually short-term, however, as the baby bumosaur would eventually outgrow the Diapersaurus and shed it, much like a snake sheds its skin. If it belonged to the Cloth species, the Diapersaurus would then move on and find a new host. If it belonged to the Disposable species, the Diapersaurus would die as soon as it was discarded.

Diapersaurus attaches itself to a newborn Bumosaur

Mature Bumosaur shedding its Diapersaurus.

cloth
diapersaurus

Diarrhoeasaurus

Extremely unpleasant in both appearance and odour, the Diarrhoeasaurus also had one of the most unpleasant life-cycles of all bumosaurs.

Due to its runny consistency, Diarrhoeasaurus was unable to pick itself up off the ground and seek shelter from the hot Triarssic sun. This meant that it was usually baked hard within hours of being born and mistaken for a crunchy snack by another unsuspecting bumosaur. After eating the toxic Diarrhoeasaurus, this bumosaur would suffer horrible stomach pains, increased gas and terrible diarrhoea. Soon after, the Diarrhoeasaurus would be expelled from the sick bumosaur's body and deposited on the ground in its liquid form once more – ready to start its life-cycle over again.

VITAL STATISTICS

Scientific name: *Puddle detestabilis*
Family: Craposaur
Diet: Unknown
Time: Triarssic 250–203 mya
Stink rating: ✿✿✿✿✿

Frill-necked cyclopootops

Named after Cyclops, the legendary one-eyed giant, the Frill-necked cyclopootops was the most glamorous member of the bumosaur family. Its huge neck frill was both a defence mechanism — making it appear larger than it actually was — and a prehistoric fashion statement.

With its long curling eyelashes, rounded cheeks and painted toenails, the Frill-necked cyclopootops had a sense of beauty and style way ahead of its time.

Although it died out with the rest of the bumosaurs at the end of the Crapaceous period, the Frill-necked cyclopootops nevertheless has been admired and worshipped by many religions and cults throughout the last 65 million years.

VITAL STATISTICS

Scientific name: *Cyclopius amazingus*
Family: Freakabutt
Diet: Fashion magazines
Time: Jurarssic, Crapaceous 203–65 mya
Stink rating: ✿ ✿ ✿ ✿ ✿

pointy
things

Skullbuttosaurus

The Skullbuttosaurus was a nocturnal bumosaur and, when it wasn't engaged in violent skull-butting contests with rival Skullbuttosauruses, it could usually be found stalking the bumtree forests at night and using its alarming appearance to scare its prey to death. At the approach of a Skullbuttosaurus, other bumosaurs would spontaneously evacuate themselves or simply drop dead with fright.

Even gigantosaurs, such as the Bigarseosaurus and the Gigantarsesaurus, were scared of the Skullbuttosaurus. As a consequence, the Skullbuttosaurus always had an abundant food supply and became very widespread by the end of the Crapaceous period.

VITAL STATISTICS

Scientific name: *Cranium enormis*
Family: Horribilosaur
Diet: Carnivorarse
Time: Jurarssic, Crapaceous 203–65 mya
Stink rating: ✿ ✿ ✿ ✿ ✿

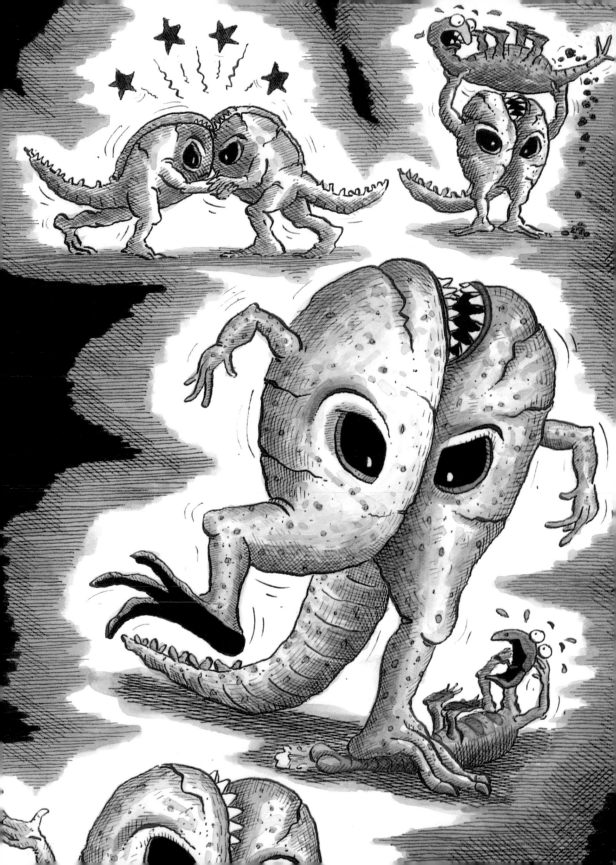

Sparebumosaurus

A passive and comparatively peaceful bumosaur, the Sparebumosaurus gets its name from the row of miniature bums sticking up from its neck, back and tail. It is thought that these bums allowed the Sparebumosaurus to replace itself in the event of a fatal accident or attack.

If a Sparebumosaurus was killed, then any of the undamaged 'spare' bums could detach themselves and grow to become exact, fully formed replicas of the dead Sparebumosaurus. If any of these new Sparebumosauruses were killed too, then their spare bums could grow into perfect replicas and so on, effectively making the Sparebumosaurus virtually indestructible.

VITAL STATISTICS

Scientific name: *Replicus arsius*
Family: Stenchosaur
Diet: Herbivorarse
Time: Jurarssic, Crapaceous 203–65 mya
Stink rating: 🌫️🌫️🌫️🌫️🌫️

rebirth of a Sparebumosaurus

miniature spare bum

Stink Kong

This huge, gorilla-like bumosaur was covered in fur except for two bare patches on the front of each of its cheeks. These were caused by its habit of pounding on itself with its fists to produce a terrifying booming sound. This pounding also served to activate its numerous stench glands to produce a terrifying stink, hence its name.

Though resembling a gorilla in appearance, Stink Kong had little else in common with modern herbivorarse, herd-dwelling apes. Stink Kong was a clumsy, stupid, aggressive loner who liked nothing better than to get involved in violent brawls with any bumosaur willing to take it on. It and the Great white bumosaurus were natural enemies and often engaged in ferocious battles that lasted for many hours.

VITAL STATISTICS

Scientific name: *Fragrantus regis*
Family: Stinkosaur
Diet: Omnivorarse
Time: Jurarssic, Crapaceous 203–65 mya
Stink rating: ✿ ✿ ✿ ✿ ✿

Toiletbrushasaurus

The Toiletbrushasaurus was the toilet cleaner of
the prehistoric bumosaur world. Not that 'toilets'
actually existed at the time – which is exactly why
the Toiletbrushasaurus played such a vital role in
prehistoric Earth's ecology.

Always in a hurry, the Toiletbrushasaurus moved
quickly. As it did so, its many strong, bristly legs
swept, cleaned and cleared the ground so that the
rest of the bumosaurs actually had somewhere to
walk instead of having to slosh around in their
own . . . well, let's just say that the average bumosaur
produced up to 20 kilograms of it a day . . . and
there were a lot of bumosaurs . . . which is probably
why the Toiletbrushasaurus was always in such a
hurry.

VITAL STATISTICS

Scientific name: *Bristilus lavatorum*
Family: Eeeuuw!osaur
Diet: Pooivorarse
Time: Jurarssic, Crapaceous 203–65 mya
Stink rating: 🟢 🟢 🟢 🟢 🟢

Tricerabutt

The Tricerabutt was a triple-cheeked bumosaur
with bony armour plating and tusk-like wart-horns
growing out of each of its cheeks.

Tricerabutts tended to form gangs of three, which
would then spend most of their time running around
looking for other gangs of Tricerabutts to attack
and stab with their horns. Drive-by hornings were
common, despite the fact that cars were not to be
invented for at least another 135 million years.

The Tricerabutt was not overly bright. Fossilized
Tricerabutt bones show that many Tricerabutts died
after running into trees, getting their horns stuck and
not being able to get them out again.

VITAL STATISTICS

Scientific name: *Tricerabuttius*
Family: Stupidosaur
Diet: Herbivorarse
Time: Jurarssic, Crapaceous 203–65 mya
Stink rating: 🐾🐾🐾🐾🐾

Tyrannosore-arse rex

There were few bumosaurs with a worse temper than
the Tyrannosore-arse rex. Driven into wild rages
by the pain in its gigantic aching cheeks, it would
rampage through the prehistoric forest, leaving
hundreds of other bumosaurs either gassed, brown-
blobbified or completely flattened.

The funny thing — or not so funny if you
happened to be a Tyrannosore-arse rex — was that
these rampages only served to make it even sorer —
and angrier — than before.

Some experts blame the Tyrannosore-arse rex
and its destructive rages for the exstinktion of many
species of small bumosaurs. Others just feel sorry for
it. Only one thing is known for sure: Tyrannosore-
arse rex had a really sore arse.

VITAL STATISTICS

Scientific name: *Soreius cheekius*
Family: Terribilosaur
Diet: Omnivorarse
Time: Jurarssic, Crapaceous 203–65 mya
Stink rating: 🌰🌰🌰🌰🌰

Bigarseosaurus

The Bigarseosaurus was so named because of its incredibly big rear end. It was so big that every time Bigarseosaurus sat down it killed at least five other smaller bumosaurs. Despite this, it was a gentle but clumsy giant that lived on the juicy leaves and bumnuts from the tops of bumnut trees.

The rear end of the Bigarseosaurus continued to expand to increasingly alarming proportions throughout the Crapaceous period, and some bumosaurologists believe that the exstinktion of the bumosaurs was due to the Bigarseosauruses' big arses becoming so big that they blotted out the sun and plunged the Earth into an extended big-arse-induced winter.

VITAL STATISTICS

Scientific name: *Superio humungarse*
Family: Gigantosaur
Diet: Herbivorarse
Time: Crapaceous 135–65 mya
Stink rating: ✿✿✿✿✿

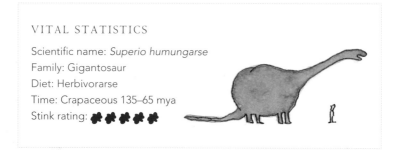

Great white bumosaurus

The Great white bumosaurus appeared on Earth towards the end of the late Crapaceous era. One of the truly gigantic bumosaurs, its most distinctive feature was its blindingly white skin. It is thought that this bioluminescence gave it a great advantage when fighting, as its incredible brightness could temporarily blind an opponent.

Some believe that the expression 'he/she thinks that the sun shines out of his/her behind' dates from the time that bumosaurologists first discovered fossil evidence of the Great white bumosaurus.

The Great white bumosaurus was also well known for its habit of dumping gigantic brown blobs on top of its enemies.

VITAL STATISTICS

Scientific name: *Maximus albinus*
Family: Disgustosaur
Diet: Omnivorarse
Time: Crapaceous 135–65 mya
Stink rating: ✿✿✿✿✿

Microbumosaurus

The Microbumosaurus was the smallest of all known bumosaurs, but it is classed as belonging to the Gigantosaur family because of its massively putrid, nostril-burning, nausea-inducing, eyebrow-singeing, throat-gagging, lung-collapsing, migraine-making, fever-causing, heart-stopping, blood-curdling, eyeball-popping stink.

With this stink, which is thought to have been caused by its exclusive diet of stinkant juice, it was capable of knocking out – and sometimes even killing – bumosaurs up to 100,000 times its size.

Small in stature, the Microbumosaurus was nevertheless enormous in impact. Some experts even speculate that the exstinktion of the bumosaurs may have been caused by a sudden explosion in the Microbumosaurus population.

VITAL STATISTICS

Scientific name: *Pongius maximus*
Family: Gigantosaur
Diet: Stinkant-juiceivorarse
Time: Crapaceous 135–65 mya
Stink rating: ✿✿✿✿✿

Stenchgantorsaurus

The Stenchgantorsaurus was one of the ugliest, dirtiest, wartiest, pimpliest, grossest, greasiest, hairiest and stinkiest of all the bumosaurs.

It is thought that it grew to be so disgusting because it lived such a long life – some specimens have been found that are thought to have had a life span of at least 400 years. And 400 years is a long time for a bum to go without being wiped. As a result, the Stenchgantorsaurus was completely blind and was one of the few bumosaurs to have a highly developed sense of smell, which it used to locate prey.

It was also prone to developing enormarse bum-pimples, which would often burst in spectacular fashion, similar in force and devarsetation to a bumcano eruption.

VITAL STATISTICS

Scientific name: *Stenchus gantori*
Family: Stenchosaur
Diet: Omnivorarse
Time: Crapaceous 135–65 mya
Stink rating: 🐾🐾🐾🐾🐾

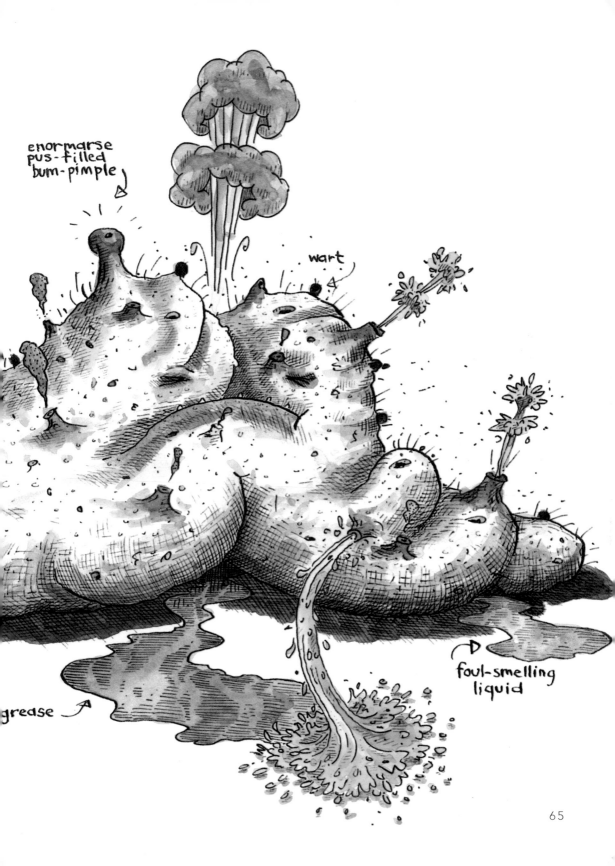

enormarse
pus-filled
bum-pimple

wart

grease

foul-smelling
liquid

Tyrannosore-arse rex versus Tricerabutt

Besides eating and fighting, there was nothing
bumosaurs liked better than eating and fighting.
And if it was fighting and eating each other,
then even better. This illarsestration is an artist's
reconstruction of an actual fight based on fossilized
remains of a Tyrannosore-arse rex and
a Tricerabutt that died mid-fight when they
were buried by a bogslide.

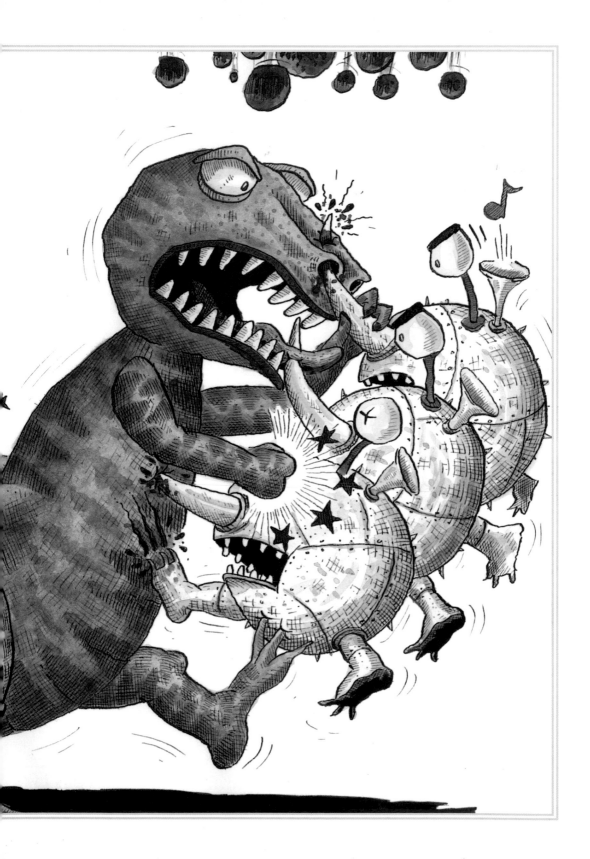

Flushasaurus rex Underpantsosaurus Bumadactyl
derpantsosaurus Bumadactyl Flushasaurus rex Un
Bumadactyl Flushasaurus rex Underpantsosaurus
hasaurus rex Underpantsosaurus Bumadactyl Flu
Underpantsosaurus Bumadactyl Flushasaurus rex
nadactyl Flushasaurus rex Underpantsosaurus Bu
hasaurus rex Underpantsosaurus Bumadactyl Flu
Underpantsosaurus Bumadactyl Flushasaurus rex
nadactyl Flushasaurus rex Underpantsosaurus Bu
Flushasaurus rex Underpantsosaurus Bumadactyl
derpantsosaurus Bumadactyl Flushasaurus rex Un
nadactyl Flushasaurus rex Underpantsosaurus Bu
Flushasaurus rex Underpantsosaurus Bumadactyl
derpantsosaurus Bumadactyl Flushasaurus rex Un
Bumadactyl Flushasaurus rex Underpantsosaurus
hasaurus rex Underpantsosaurus Bumadactyl Flu
Underpantsosaurus Bumadactyl Flushasaurus rex
nadactyl Flushasaurus rex Underpantsosaurus Bu
Flushasaurus rex Underpantsosaurus Bumadactyl
derpantsosaurus Bumadactyl Flushasaurus rex Un
Bumadactyl Flushasaurus rex Underpantsosaurus
hasaurus rex Underpantsosaurus Bumadactyl Flu
Underpantsosaurus Bumadactyl Flushasaurus rex
nadactyl Flushasaurus rex Underpantsosaurus Bu
Flushasaurus rex Underpantsosaurus Bumadactyl
derpantsosaurus Bumadactyl Flushasaurus rex Un
Bumadactyl Flushasaurus rex Underpantsosaurus
hasaurus rex Underpantsosaurus Bumadactyl Flu
Underpantsosaurus Bumadactyl Flushasaurus rex
nadactyl Flushasaurus rex Underpantsosaurus Bu
Flushasaurus rex Underpantsosaurus Bumadactyl

Bumornithids

As competition on the land became ever keener some of the bumosaurs began to take advantage of the thrusting power of their gas emissions and launched themselves into the air. Others supplemented their gas power with large saggy flaps of skin, which they used as primitive wings, and gradually learned to master controlled flight.

BUMADACTYL

FLUSHASAURUS REX

UNDERPANTSOSAURUS

Bumadactyl

The Bumadactyl was one of the first bums to take to the air. It had a vast wing-span of 50m, but its 'wings' were actually nothing more than large, loose, leathery flaps of bumcheek skin, and it gained most of its lift and speed from its abundant gas power.

Unfortunately, the Bumadactyl was at the mercy of its primitive, crudely formed bowels and would often go out of control, like a balloon that is blown up and then let go without its end being tied.

Clogging the skies during the late Triarssic period, Bumadactyls were largely responsible for the creation of the methane layer in the Earth's atmosphere.

VITAL STATISTICS

Scientific name: *Cheekum flaparsius*
Family: Flapposaurid
Diet: Carnivorarse
Time: Messozoic era 250–203 mya
Stink rating: ✿✿✿✿✿

Bumadactyl flies out of control after gas explosion

Flushasaurus rex

The Flushasaurus rex was not an ancient predecessor of the modern flush toilet as is often thought. In fact, despite sharing the same basic shape, they are not related at all.

The Flushasaurus rex had wings, legs and a barbed tail. Modern flush toilets have none of these. Another major difference is that the Flushasaurus rex did not dispose of waste like a modern toilet, but instead spent most of its time hurling great loads of dirty, smelly water out of its mouth. This was done in self-defence, as other bumosaurs were always trying to sit on it, which was probably due to the extreme shortage of modern flush toilets on Earth during the reign of the bumosaurs.

VITAL STATISTICS

Scientific name: *Vomitus projectilius*
Family: Freakasaurid
Diet: Carnivorarse
Time: Jurarssic 203–135 mya
Stink rating: ✿ ✿ ✿ ✿ ✿

Underpantsosaurus

Underpantsosauruses mostly travelled in pairs, though they sometimes formed large groups known as multipacks. These multipacks sometimes contained so many Underpantsosauruses that they would form a cloud thick enough to block out the sun. Events such as these struck fear into the hearts of land-dwelling bumosaurs, which could imagine nothing worse than being trapped inside a big dirty stinky smelly pair of Underpantsosauruses.

Unlike most bumosaurs, the Underpantsosaurus did not die out completely, but rather bumvolved over many millions of years, becoming gradually smaller and more fashionable. During this process of bumolution the Underpantsosaurus lost its ability to fly and the more modern species were eventually domesticated by bum-men and kept in underpants drawers.

VITAL STATISTICS

Scientific name: *Jockus maximus*
Family: Knickersaurid
Diet: Carnivorarse
Time: Jurarssic 203–135 mya
Stink rating:

ess Num-monster Disgustagong Great w
isgustagong Great woolly butthead Bumanderth
utthead Bumanderthal Loch Ness bum-monster
Ness bum-monster Disgustagong Great woolly buttl
reat woolly butthead Bumanderthal Loch Ne
umanderthal Loch Ness bum-monster Disgustago
onster Disgustagong Great woolly butthead Bur
oolly butthead Bumanderthal Loch Ness bum-mc
och Ness bum-monster Disgustagong Great w
isgustagong Great woolly butthead Bumanderth
utthead Bumanderthal Loch Ness bum-monster
Ness bum-monster Disgustagong Great woolly buttl
reat woolly butthead Bumanderthal Loch Ne
umanderthal Loch Ness bum-monster Disgustago
onster Disgustagong Great woolly butthead Bur
oolly butthead Bumanderthal Loch Ness bum-mc
och Ness bum-monster Disgustagong Great w
isgustagong Great woolly butthead Bumanderth
utthead Bumanderthal Loch Ness bum-monster
Ness bum-monster Disgustagong Great woolly buttl
reat woolly butthead Bumanderthal Loch Ne
umanderthal Loch Ness bum-monster Disgustago
onster Disgustagong Great woolly butthead Bur
oolly butthead Bumanderthal Loch Ness bum-mc
och Ness bum-monster Disgustagong Great w
isgustagong Great woolly butthead Bumanderth
utthead Bumanderthal Loch Ness bum-monster
Ness bum-monster Disgustagong Great woolly buttl
reat woolly butthead Bumanderthal Loch Ne
umanderthal Loch Ness bum-monster Disgustago
onster Disgustagong Great woolly butthead Bur
oolly butthead Bumanderthal Loch Ness bum-mc

Bummals

While a few bumosaurs may have survived the mass exstinktion at the end of the Crapaceous period, the relative absence of bumosaurs created opportunities for the bumolution of prehistoric bummals, which led to the development of Bumanderthals and their descendants, the earliest bum-men (also known as humans).

LOCH NESS BUM-MONSTER

DISGUSTAGONG

GREAT WOOLLY BUTTHEAD

BUMANDERTHAL

Loch Ness
bum-monster

The most famarse deep-water dwelling bummal is
the Loch Ness bum-monster, which for hundreds
of years has been reported to inhabit Loch Ness, an
extraordinarily deep lake in Botland.

    Evidence for the existence of this species is almost
exclusively in the form of eyewitness accounts.
People have reported seeing a bum or series of bums
and an extremely long neck with a bum-shaped head
rising from the water's surface.

    The only piece of evidence that both experts and
non-experts agree is one hundred per cent reliable
is this picture of the Loch Ness bum-monster by
world-famarse bumosaurologist, Jock MacDouglarse,
who has seen and drawn the mysterious creature on
at least three separate occasions.

VITAL STATISTICS

Scientific name: *Monsteri rectumius*
Family: Mysteriosaur
Diet: Unknown
Time: Perhaps Sewerian 435 mya to present
Stink rating: Unknown

Disgustagong

One of the most disgusting of all sea-going bummals, the Disgustagong had disgusting, stumpy little flippers and a disgusting, stupid-looking face and spent its time doing disgusting things like ~~picking its nose~~ and ~~eating it~~ and sometimes even ~~feeding it to its friends!~~

It could also often be heard making disgusting noises such as ~~purpfartburp!~~, ~~squelchgarglesquish~~, ~~phlegmcoughsnallowd!~~, and ~~ed-up bumweed'~~. But the most disgusting thing of all about the Disgustagong was when it vomited up bu~~mweed~~ ~~vomited it up again~~ and ~~baked it into a new cake,~~ ~~etc., so. Baked it into a new cak~~e all day long!

NOTE: The above passage has had certain lines blacked out because they are too disgusting for anyone to read.

VITAL STATISTICS

Scientific name: *Disgustaceous enormi*
Family: Bummal
Diet: ~~Snotvomitiv~~orarse
Time: Fartocene 65–1.75 mya
Stink rating: ❧❧❧❧❧

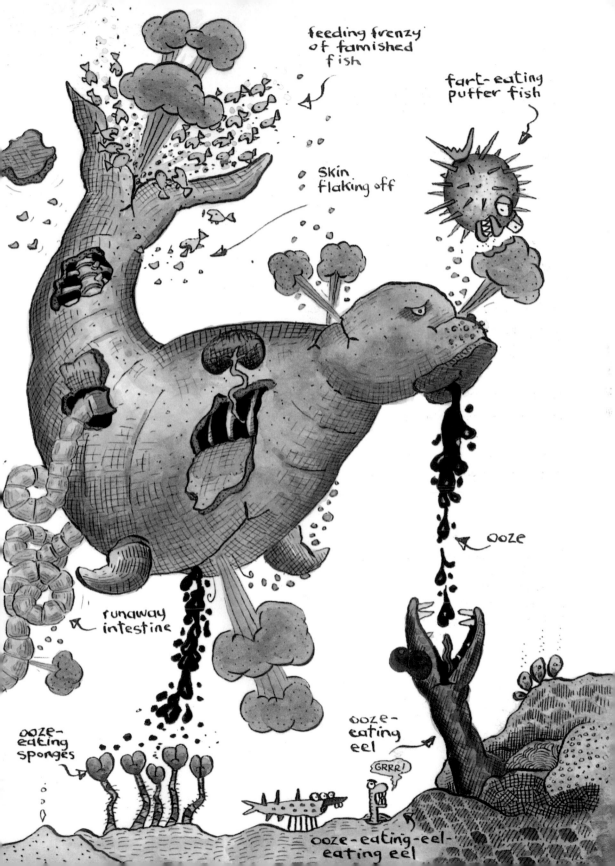

Great woolly butthead

Despite its vacant stare and less than flattering name, the Great woolly butthead was actually one of the most intelligent of the post-bumosaur Scentozoic era bummals, thanks to its two brains, located in its twin-cheeked forehead.

Admittedly, its thoughts, e.g. 'Why does everybody call me a butthead?' and 'What's for dinner?', could never be mistaken for those of a great philosopher. Nevertheless, this was thinking of an almost Einsteinian complexity compared to the 'thoughts' that had drifted occasionally through the tiny brown blobs that served as 'brains' for the average bumosaur, e.g. 'Stink', 'Kill', 'Eat', 'Wipe', 'Stink'.

VITAL STATISTICS

Scientific name: *Hirsutus cranium*
Family: Bummal
Diet: Herbivorarse
Time: Bumocene 1.75 mya – present
Stink rating: ✿✿✿✿✿

Bumanderthal

With their bottoms vastly reduced in size, modern bum-men represent the triumph of brain over bum, but with three bums – one behind, one on top and one in front – Bumanderthal man was still more bum than brain. Relatively primitive and unintelligent creatures, they nevertheless tried their best to communicate with each other, but their early attempts at language were hampered by mid-sentence eruptions of large quantities of gas, rude noises and solid matter.

With three bums to look after, however, Bumanderthals were obsessed with the quest for a softer toilet paper, and many bumolutionists now believe that this drive was largely responsible for the subsequent growth of the brain and, in turn, the rise of modern civilization.

VITAL STATISTICS

Scientific name: *Homo rectumus*
Family: Bummal
Diet: Omnivorarse
Time: Bumocene 1.75 mya – present
Stink rating: ✿✿✿✿✿

Exstinktion of the bumosaurs

There are many theories as to what caused the exstinktion of the bumosaurs, but the most likely explanation is the collision of a giant arseteroid with the Earth around 65 million years ago. It probably looked something like this:

A selected list of titles available from Macmillan Children's Books

The prices shown below are correct at the time of going to press. However, Macmillan Publishers reserves the right to show new retail prices on covers, which may differ from those previously advertised.

Andy Griffiths

Just Annoying!	978-0-330-39729-2	£4.99
Just Crazy!	978-0-330-39729-8	£4.99
Just Disgusting!	978-0-330-41592-7	£4.99
Just Kidding!	978-0-330-39728-5	£4.99
Just Stupid!	978-0-330-39726-1	£4.99
The Day My Bum Went Psycho	978-0-330-40089-3	£4.99
Zombie Bums from Uranus	978-0-330-43680-9	£4.99
Bumageddon . . . The Final Pongflict	978-0-330-43370-9	£4.99

Frank Cottrell Boyce

Framed	978-0-330-43425-6	£5.99
Millions	978-0-330-43331-0	£5.99

All Pan Macmillan titles can be ordered from our website, www.panmacmillan.com, or from your local bookshop and are also available by post from:

Bookpost, PO Box 29, Douglas, Isle of Man IM99 IBQ
Credit cards accepted. For details:
Telephone: 01624 677237
Fax: 01 624 670923
Email: bookshop@enterprise.net
www.bookpost.co.uk

Free postage and packing in the United Kingdom